# Beautiful. And Ugly Too

Poems by

## M.K. Asante, Jr.

## Africa World Press, Inc.

P.O. Box 1892
Trenton, NJ 08607

P.O. Box 48
Asmara, ERITREA

## Africa World Press, Inc.

P.O. Box 1892
Trenton, NJ 08607

P.O. Box 48
Asmara, ERITREA

First Printing 2005

Cover and Book design: Dapo Ojo-Ade

Front and Back Cover photography: Bill Hayward

Library of Congress Cataloging-in-Publication Data

Asante, Molefi K., 1981-
  Beautiful. And ugly too: poems / by M.K. Asante, Jr.
    p. cm.
  ISBN 1-59221-421-5 — ISBN 1-59221-422-3 (pbk.)
  1. African Americans—Poetry. I. Title.

PS3601.S26B43 2005
811'.6—dc22

2005022931

*With gratitude toward my parents & mentors,*
*in memory of Nkosi Johnson,*
*and for Maya.*

*We younger Negro artists who create now intend to express our individual dark-skinned selves without fear or shame. If white people are pleased we are glad. If they are not, it doesn't matter... The tom-tom cries and the tom-tom laughs. If colored people are pleased we are glad. If they are not, their displeasure doesn't matter either... We know we are beautiful. And ugly too.*

— Langston Hughes

# Table Of Contents

S>he ............................................................ 1

Seeing Red ................................................. 2

Zimbassippi ................................................ 4

The Luxury of Ignorance: Based on Shock & Awe .............. 5

Regarding Nananoam .................................. 8

Fragrance of an Invisible Flower ......................... 9

The Spirit of Nkosi Johnson .......................... 10

The Master's Mother Tongue, Mastered by My Mother ... 12

Beautiful. And Ugly Too ............................... 13

A Beat Sentence ........................................... 17

Imagined Nation ......................................... 18

One of the Ways God Must Taste ................... 19

I am not that Random, America .................... 20

SAMO© ....................................................... 22

A Scene from Sinema Noir ........................... 24

Grandmother ............................................... 26

I, Too .......................................................... 27

Convenient Season ...................................... 28

Maafa .......................................................... 29

The Essential Americans .............................. 30

Live, Afro-Bohemian: A Tribute to Afrobohemianism ...... 31

British Museum Blues ................................... 33

Thicker Than Blood ...................................... 34

Public School ............................................... 35

Father ................................................................... 36

Ghetto Booty: The Hottentot Remix ...................................... 38

Missing ................................................................. 40

Miles Smiles (Circle) .................................................. 41

Elderly Race Leaders ................................................... 42

On the Poetree of Phyllis Wheatley: My Great, Great

  Babymomma ............................................................ 43

Clipped-Wing Birds ..................................................... 44

Notes .................................................................. 45

# A Libation in the Dark Tradition

*Dark tradition means a lot more than*
*black tradition. There is a lot of division*
*in what they call black. I'm not into*
*division, I'm into coordination, discipline*
*and precision.*

— Sun-Ra

We call upon our ancestors

     – far and near, mothers of our mothers, and
fathers of our fathers –

to lend pure compassion,
extend limbs of courtesy,
deliver us from the care-
less,

to expose us to freedom,
grace our remembrance,
illuminate our wasteful-
ness,

and to rend our mercy,
so that we may sleep –
in order to wake.

Amen.

# S>he

*for Maya Freelon*

It's the battery of love
against water and above earth, &
underneath it all lies that silent validation
of cliché's, pearl-strung across the tan neck of She;
the great laureate of modern femininity & untranslatables
captured from sketches of bright tongues lost in
forgotteness.

And it's like when God
revealed herself to the almighty
Professor of Nothing at the University of
Tailored Intellects & Tragic Greek Letters, who
despite his re-re-regurgitations of archaic pale logic,
couldn't muster words which amounted to an
overstanding of anything real.

She was just like that.


*(Paris)*

M.K. Asante, Jr.

# Seeing Red

*There is no place on this earth*
*without my fingerprint, and*
*my heel upon the skeleton of*
*skyscrapers, and my sweat in*
*the brilliance of diamonds.*
— Aimé Cesairé

It's denying the existence of absolute beauty, &
daring to see past the masqueraded figureheads
who-be, unscrupulously, in Waldorf Astoria
asking to jack-off Jackson or impatiently waiting
to swallow Franklin.

Who all own *sumptin*, in addition to the means, yet
neglect questioning the meaning of production.

In a colorful sudden;

The lights – in the city of them – quench
from imperial stench, as the
statued, stolen races, held captive in grand,
London-fogged museums, reveal their sullen
faces. And in the distance,

American trails shed red tears for those
who were not discovered, as the

thick lashes that replaced wages resound
beneath the disrobed and uncovered.

It is;

Seeing email as the numerical bombs their creators sought and the oxymoron of imposed democracy as certainly bossed and bought.
Seeing red demands below-the-surface thought.

For it is not mere knowledge, it's knowing-the-ledge, and observing all his stories beauty from underneath the bleeding edge.

*(Paris)*

# Zimbassippi

In a box of a space between imagined lines,
stood the gold-thumbed prints,
which before my time,

inhaled the thin,
unbroken-in,
darkened
limbs of
kin,

while grandelders hymned,
her and him,
them,

into the mud-thatched banks of our golden
conch/us/nest, which nourished
our pain,

and ignited grains of thought into glass-shattering
epiphanies of re: mining Midtown
shining Tiffany's,

asking simply, for her stone-history's Achilles.


*(Harare)*

4

# The Luxury of Ignorance:
# Based on Shock & Awe

Planes fly.
Thousands die.

Planes fly.
Thousands die.

Planes fly
Thousands die.

But why them planes fly?
Why them thousands die?

I'll watch CNN's spin
over and over again, like
Herc when rap began —
until I think America is
sin-free.

Or

perhaps MSNBC'll transform
me into a one man military,
waging neo-con-jihad on
the axis of the *evil-doer enemy.*

I'll draw a line,
not well defined,
barely outlined;
  *You either with us or them* – visible to the blind, from
behind.
All because they hate America's

freedom & way of life, right?

Those crazy extremist, militants,
radicals, ant-Israelites, right?

Those sand niggers hate American democracy.

Dune-coons hating on our American democracy.

But, what about American ~~foreign policies~~?

Exploiting children in Indonesia,
collapsing Argentina.

Summarily bombing Sudan,
Libya, Somalia, Nicaragua, Haiti, Afghanistan.

Raping South African diamond mines?

What about shhhhh...
Palestine?

It is my belief, to no relief, that they'd like
Us to believe that;

> Islamic militants, forced to the stench
> & confinement of concentration tents,
> denied aid from the American government,
> and made 2nd class citizens,
> > *blow themselves up because they're crazy.*

And we, quite naïve, do believe,
baptized by the pixels of BSTV.

Unable to see
the planes that will continue to fly or
the thousands that will ultimately die, as long as

*how, how many, what, where, and with whom*
give economic asylum to

WHY.

A War On Terrorism is a postmodern way of saying
we are waging a war against ourselves: semi Colin,
the wealthiest nation as a result of
terrorist occupations. Infused with

corporate scenes in evil acts, in the theatrical-conquest
that – with careful manipulation – can move from

*nigger to negro to black, as seamlessly as Bin Laden to Afghan to Iraq.*

Yes Them — same ones that did that to Arafat.
Oil dinosaurs with blood-shot pours
lying under their fiery pristine dream,

neglecting the meaning of production.

The luxury of ignorance is something.

M.K. Asante, Jr.

# Regarding Nananom[*]

I studied them,
mouthing homeless.

Their aloneness told me
they had traveled,

a dilapidated jitney
unraveled a path probably

via no place to be somebody,
into the paved perils of city,

and pity they'd become
dusky Western-dwellers.

.        Regarding nananom;

before *them*, not them,
there were no sellers.


(*El Mina*)

---

[*] Twi: Ancestors.

# Fragrance of an Invisible Flower

> *Look at this surprising flower*
> *which cannot be seen, and yet its*
> *fragrance cannot be hidden.*
> — Bhauddin Valad

Beautiful broken pedals pose against
sweaty summer air like brown rebels,
reveling in the thirsty gardens of an
unpollinated ghetto.

Junoesque stems challenge the power of
gusted winds, like the women of Cain
toward the chain jewelry fencing their
sun's in.

Soil stands in the cloth of mulch without
rooted substrata, like the thorned roses
which arose from the muddy banks of our
torn Diaspora.

Hereafter;

I bare witness to the flowers I ignored
in my childhood – as a child would.

Blind to the wax-mold which encased
the gold that informed the soul of
a corn-rowed code that spoke
truth to power,

through the vehicle that bent
toward the sun, revealing
the flower.

M.K. Asante, Jr.

# The Spirit of Nkosi Johnson

*Care for us and accept us, we are*
*all human beings, we are normal*
*we have hands, we have feet, we*
*can walk, we can talk, we have*
*needs just like everyone else, don't*
*be afraid of us – we are the same.*
— Nkosi Johnson

Who was the child that smiled at sorrow
and spoke Struggle fluently?

The child with the victory of humanity
wrinkled into the skin of his spirit.

Who pleaded, *do all you can, with what you have,*
*in the time you have, in the place you are.*

The child who was sick because we were.
Who gave until, when and after it hurt.

The living embodiment of what must be God;
                    Anyone's. Anywhere. Everywhere.

Who poured the life-force of love into the empty
valves of our souls, just to recruit our hearts.

The child of the sun, who bathed in its rays so that
splashes of light might spatter-up, and wash our fears
away.

Who wasn't allowed to age – so he evolved, responding to the sacred challenge of being human.

The child whose knees denied the quakes of harping on even the most positive of fates.

Who, at half the size of nothing, was the iron-skin orchestra of the seen, unseen, and those incapable of being seen.

The child whose wide-eyes, pressed against his face like the creator's emblem, belonged to the future;
Yours. Mine. Ours.

Have you ever witnessed the balm of the remarkable?

Listened to the modest echoes of the inspirational?
Felt the yen of pristine compassion?
Or – even for a moment – touched the fountain of living waters?

For if you have, then you know.
And because you know, you too, must love.

The child that was –
IS.

M.K. Asante, Jr.

# The Master's Mother Tongue, Mastered by My Mother

*You taught me language, and my*
*profit on't is, I know how to*
*curse. The red plague rid you for*
*learning me your language!*
                            — Caliban

In a steady, singular breath,
my mother and master uttered
warring marks of
ink.

As I, a native son on a dusky
island of women, attempted to
breakinguish the
link,

between a second and a first,
a gift and a curse.


*(Kingston)*

# Beautiful. And Ugly Too

**I.**

Beauty born mourning sunset,
but the beautyful ones ain't born,
yet.

(barely audible) *Yes they is.*

They is?

*M-hm*

Where?

(clasping hands)

Serving a sleeping sentence?

Well then, wake'em up –
tell'em "we got dreams to finish."

And we ain't got all day.

It says.

*Who says?*

We say,

today because yesterday is through
and tomorrow…

...well, keep it up,
tomrrow'll be gone, too.

But be cool.
Be real cool.
                    *Who real cool?*
We at least 'reel cool.'

And

we real beautiful.
                    *Ugly, too.*


**II.**


Blood skin, eyes green.

Fine history,
            salt & tweed.

The elephant Tuskeg of

Montgomery *boom-bap* seeds

unable to redeem the dream
of what somewhat said look
like him.

                    *Might could be, born again.*

**III.**

And,
what if it had turned-up heads?

Turns out: "It did," she said.

> *I can't tell.*

**IV.**

&

Where the hell are the best
mines of my generation?

> (?)

A post hip-hop nation's
starmap of Capetown
play stations,

pirated from darkwater
basements,
adjacent to

no place to be somebody.

**V.**

It was probably White folks.

Couldn't been us.

What?

> *T'was.*

Well then – we learned it from them.

*When?*

The last time we did the blame dance.

Shall we?

(exhausted) *Again?*

**VI.**

Question:

How do you give birth to a nation that
was never pregnant?

Like resurrecting Indians who
ain't dead yet.

I stay awake and wonder
if the Black middle class is just White folks'
subset?

&

If the Asian-American identity, post-Clorox,
will have anything left?

*Only what's left.*

**VII.**

The beautyful ones ain't born yet.

# A Beat Sentence

*for Sambo & Others*

Teardrops of rain
fell and flickered like old film,
before *tap tap tap*
against the pane;

      like troupes of chicken-chasers with happy feet's
      and swarthy residue, nigger-black and neat,

      from burnt corks named Dartmouth and Rastus
      who, with vaudeville grins, asked us to

      shiftlessly lay heel iron on wood tables where the
      torn, barely visible but clearly labeled

flyers without revision,
read 'evil, lazy and knows-his-place,'
before, after and during
bouts of intermission.


*(Hollywood)*

# Imagined Nation

Imagined nation,
running free like ink dreams,
hiding in the wrinkled minds of the
thieves who swallow the dry innocence of
the unseen.

They are now visible. Young and gifted, but
divisible, staggering through streets where
riddled shots, sickle cells, and cityPD's pursue
faster then the heartbeats of archetypal black
athletes.

And papers, preachers too, scream hopeless,
as they struggle defining what hope is.

Forcing our retreat into the night, where we
bargain with death for discounts on life;
we get:

     HALF OFF!

By twenty were scattered to systems;
education, corporate, and all the ism's, which
without vision, act as prisons. Narrowing our

perspective, freedom cannot be an elective,
attending schools boasting most selective
when, quite selectively, ourstory is neglected.

Drowned in dharma, like rotting pieces of wood
while we shoot yet another movie glory frying the hood.
Giving them, and us, window seats to confirm
our defeat, and all we can say is *I'm tryna eat.*
    Imagine fasting.

*(Compton)*

# One of the Ways God Must Taste

> *Scratch the surface of reality and*
> *you will discover God. We, in fact,*
> *discover the Oneness of Being by*
> *staying right here.*
> — Arthur Green

Beneath the ebb of the dying,
    it lives.

Pull-back the foreskin of existence
    to reveal its head.

Scratch the surface of a record
    and hear it talk in tongues.

Interrogate the fiery pages of
    invisible flowers & unseen rain.

Talk to seer Ginsberg about the
    children of the night.

Dig through the evolution of corpses in
    search of the light you stand upon.

The what was,
    is, and will-be aroma of the concealed,
    until Her face, wrinkled with obvious
miracles, is revealed.

*(Washington Heights)*

M.K. Asante, Jr.

# I am not that Random, America

*For the ambiguously ethnic*

I am not that random, America;
my passport is the earth-tone of
your ambitious itinerary.

I am not that random, America;
recognize me from ventures
in the featureless desert.

I am not that random, America;
I built this shiny airport
by lying down & dying.

I am not that random, America;
you beam me syndication & I
laugh – to keep from crying.

I am not that random, America;
you searched the pockets of my
native tongue for spare grammar.

I am not that random, America;
the lyrics of your dream are the
soundtracks of my workday.

I am not that random, America;
I subscribe to your magazines
just to read the pictures.

I am not that random, America;
I, too, sing songs of pain and
remembrance. Remember?

Perhaps you were too young to.

But America, I am not black.
           — What is it with all these questions?
What am I?

I am that curious shade of brown
that conjures either a red past of guilt
or a sandy future or terror.
           Or both.

America,
do you know why I'm at your gates?

           — What is it with all these questions?
I'm here on business, for the third time.

America,
you said this would only take a minute.

Do you know what time it is?
Your eyes:

half-distain,
half-trained,
interrogate my belongings in patriotic tantrums.

You gave birth to me, America.
&
I am not that random.

M.K. Asante, Jr.

# SAMO©

*For Jean-Michel Basquiat*

The History of Black People –
how much time you got?

A couple more than 25 to *his*life,

barely none, and not enough
to cross-out enough words to obscure
enough ideas that wasn't crossed-out
enough so we could read them.

And the fact that they was crossed-out
made you want to read them, *right*?

A shiny quarter later and a
torn, stolen two dollar bill after –
what comes after is SAMO, *right*?

Not the one that tells cave-dogs to slobber
on the skin-sleeves of dark people, or the
kind that hide Graffiti behind glass, or truly
believe they own drops of waterearth.

No;

SAMO is the end – to mind wash theosophy,
nowhere politics & bogus order, playing art,
tailored intellectuals with unlived accents,
cars that must change, television sex,
pseudo-emotion over-flowing, and

the search for god's name on the inside of overpriced cotton.

Can't you see where this is going?

*(Brooklyn)*

M.K. Asante, Jr.

# A Scene from Sinema Noir

FADE IN on
the tragedy (in) the film.

> The ESTABLISHING SHOT reveals
> BERT WILLIAMS, abbreviated *nigger* bellhop,
> who...
>
> Spins, grins, and dances,
> however he doesn't advance our plot. So we...
>
> CUT TO an all *colored* cast, vaselined, singing
> to cotton ears, waiting for the sun to pass. CUT
> TO...
>
> a CLOSE UP of Stepin, tumbling his eyes,
> head bowed to teach the girl with the truest, bluest
> eye, the burnt cork adolescence, lesson. Brown
> eyes...
>
> DISSOLVE into the lens of pasted prible pages. And
> we snatch traces – it's the master's mother tongue,
> mastered by my mother:
>
> > "I yam what I yam."
>
> We PAN the hills, gliding over devoted watermelon
> seeds, stuck between the windmills of glossy-
> vehicled reels for the song-and-dance-man – tuh
> dans mahn.
>
> And to, with oily face, sing-a-song bout knowing-
> his-place, then suddenly we ZOOM IN on the...

CHASE; *a tragic mulatto followed by a dark, barefoot brute, who's followed by a flapjack cook in zoot suit, who's sweating, running from a chicken-chaser, clothed in soot,* then suddenly the pursuit...

SLOWS, and we PULL BACK, just beyond OSCAR MICHEAUX, to watch the absurd, broken, poor ole Joe prose of – and this is why it hurts – someone who actually knows.

> "I jest know you is outdoor man –
> you is so sunburned, come in Sinner,
> and be washed whiter than snow.
> Come from the kiln."

FADE OUT on
the tragedy (of) the film.

# Grandmother

Trees must have blown wind
into your belly to begin
again. And

I arrive at this place again,
and again, swallowing cupped
conviction through the brass
straw of womanhood.

Grandmother of the supernatural,
veins of leonine crushed into your
tough smile.

Your bones, already in heaven, rose
to the mediumship of our eyes,
fixated on manifestations of victory.


*(Cairo)*

# I, Too

I, too,
walk
- by and buy -
the basement which is desire;
        the Americana labor of
firebranded quicksand.

It's shiny: *perhaps it'll reely
define me?* So-so shiny.

It does for my man-purse what
soda does for my thirst; q –
wench.

It's Los Angeles; home to the
cancerous brand evangelists...

```
    *  *  *
    *  S  *
    *  h  *
    *  o  *
    *  p  *
    *  *  *
```

Will terrorism stop?

*I, too* – (sniffle)
bless you.

## Convenient Season

Given away to the falling water of your name
amid the orange clay of change, when we
upstaged the pane with water paint;

to make burnished yellows and reds, smeared in
the grimace of Chimurenga rose fields, re-
pressed against oxide from coal shields.

&

an isolated pyramid, built with stones unheard,
edged with earth, dangles from the out
stretched neck of a sun-golden bird,

its beak bent back,

its eyes; star maps
of the way forward,
superimposed atop five points of Shonglish prose.

The orphan is a king,
like the soil that everyone steps on.

# Maafa*

As darkness covers the night sky,
lullabies subdue cries and

crash tides against the face of the coast,
breathed by the children of the most

high. And as night creeps-by,
for the Them and They taken away

on coffin-floats, we sings songs of
human hope

soaked with the determination to
be unlost and go fetch it,

the *wretched of the earth* have been
baptized by the

painful demise of alien paradigms
that compete for the mines of our

hearts, which suffering has opened.

And our songs are the oceans that
have touched the shores of humanity.

And not living in the sadness of
inverted vision is our sanity.


*(Abu Simbel)*

---

* Kiswahili: Terrible occurrence.

M.K. Asante, Jr.

# The Essential Americans

Us is the hidden instruments
of rustling cotton flags.

The authentic beatniks, though
we don't call it that;

> those natural knacks emanating from the naps
> under the wool hats that cover the *boom baps* in our
> minds. Sure,

S'how come we don't need music
to keep colored peoples time.

And I'm still waiting for          colored          peoples
time.

Us is the automatic hipster,
the affinity of the world's fantasy-identity,
without the garb of freedom, of course.

And our coarse is jazz;

> We yawn blues.
> Mumble scats.
> Whisper soul.
> Walk tap.
> Cry spirituals.
> And Spit raps.
> But

we live and we die, and *this* has everything to do with *that*.

# Live, Afrobohemian:
# A Tribute to Afrobohemianism

*They've got this government of the*
*people, by the people and for the*
*people. They didn't include me. I'm*
*a leader, I'm not the people.*

— Sun-Ra

Live, Afrobohemian;
> for the poet laureates of Valdosta cotton fields, and
> the white men trapped in Pennsylvania steel mills.

Live, Afrobohemian;
> for the spirit-quench tinge of forgiveness, and
> the concrete abdomen of yesternow's emptiness.

Live, Afrobohemian;
> for the unposterizing of your bearded ancestors,
> frightened at the thought of desolate semesters.

Live, Afrobohemian;
> for the bourgeoisie existence of your nine-to-five
> parents, it is those same hours which have
> stretched your canvas.

Live, Afrobohemian;
> for the sand-glazed children, lost in Sudan, and
> the garments of flesh, scattered 'cross torn land.

Live, Afrobohemian;
> for skies wearing rainbows as belts to keep clouds
> high, hands separate, music dripping from the
> watery eye.

Live, Afrobohemian;
    Somewhere absent from the monogamous routine,
    just visible enough to exploit the fruits of
    mainstream.

Live, Afrobohemian;
    Neosoul of college township colonization
    and the dark diesel of sudden gentrification.

Live, Afrobohemian;
    Troubadour of the North Philadelphia voice,
    volunteer of poverty – afforder of choice.

Live, Afrobohemian;
    Moral mirror of the middle class and trite,
    making passion life, and seizing the value-card
    from the right.

Live, Afrobohemian;
    Under the floating nationality of dashiki prose,
    matted beneath the fiery locks of jagged 'fros.

Live Afrobohemian;
    For the Them not allowed to;

    Penbrush the margins, Afrobohem,
    if not – then who?

*(Dakar)*

# British Museum Blues

Pharaoh, you've been gone for so long,
I forgot, but been meaning,
to sing Dis* song.

See, this museum better be free,
least for all the folks who got
tone like me.

Cause when I look around,
mahn, that's all I see.

All thieving is wrong, no matter
what nobody do or say,

especially when you dig folks'
family-up, to put'em on display.

British blues and union jacks
why not send the stolen goods back?

The mummies, the art, & even the pearls
that way folks could truly see the world.

So that's my story,
all I got to spare,

let's free the frozen prisoners
trapped in Russell Square.

(*London*)

---

* Biblical: Capital of Hell.

M.K. Asante, Jr.

# Thicker Than Blood

They ask me to look at the numbers,
so much so that I see them in my sleep.

Gasping across the sky of my dreams,
under the blue yarn of my sheets.

Deep-fried hands counting decimal heads,
separating the dark end from the digits
descent on that *ole wooden waterbed*.

And then I saw them.

And the numbers, like the once blazon cuts
stitched into the tough man's arm,

fade into the vague dream of something
gone.

# Public School

*For those unable to distinguish*

Ni ruo smaerd, ew evah sseltimil
secruoser dna eht elpoep dleiy sevles-
meht htiw tcefrep ytilicod ot ruo gnidlom
sdnah.

Eht tneserp noitacude snoitnevnoc edaf
morf rieht sdnim, dna derepmahnu yb
noitidart, ew krow ruo now doog lliw
nopu a lufetarg dna evisnopser larur klof.

Ew llahs ton yrt ot ekam eseht elpoep ro
yna fo rieht nerdlihc otni nem fo gninrael.

Ew evah ton ot esiar pu morf gnoma meht
srohtua, srotide, steop, ro nem fo srettel.

Eht ksat ew tes erofeb sevlesruo si yrev elpmis
sa llew sa a yrev beautiful eno, ot niart eseht
elpoep sa ew dnif meht ot a yltcefrep laedi
life,
        just where they are.

M.K. Asante, Jr.

# Father

*For his mother*

I pitch this in darkness for my father whom I seldom saw,
yet who gave me courage to fail for a Cause;

Who spoke of the mighty meaning of morning days,
turning my face towards its early rays;

Who wasn't afraid of the night, professing that the gift of
death was the sweet aftertaste of life;

Whose holy fingers knew the Moses-cotton in southern
shirts, and when the load was heavy, said *work the work;*

Who knew redemption's cost, maintaining a wretched
school year could be saved in May, preventing total loss;

Who was staunch in his stance, belittling the deeds of his
days as a lens to pull focus from self-arrogance;

Who was careful on rest-day, not to destroy his hardnoble-
work with contradictory play.

Who put Esther-women first, confessing that male-
dominance was indeed a barbarous curse.

Who not only lived within his means, but never flaunted
colors or ribbons in the face of those in need;

Whose sensitivity blessed the meek, able to hear the cries
of the struggling grass beneath the trample of our

thoughtless feet;

Who pulled smiles from pouts, good from evil, us from them, and determination from doubts;

Whose desire for fruition burned, and who scolded me for wishing rest before rest was earned;

Who spoke of the glorious day we'd step into life, or at least out of idle- and empty-rife;

Whose religion was expressed in his tasks, through caution and balance, he sankofaed for his past;

Who, through his candor always chose less, and knew that honest failure was far greater than stolen success;

Who forbid me to ever borrow, teaching the children of today to ensure a better tomorrow;

Who preached that pride in our race and state, without the same wish for others, is a pride raised in mistake;

Who measure life not by failure's probability, but by the infiniteness of human possibility;

Whose fearlessness rested upon the confidence of the ultimate right, and to physical hurt or unpopularity – he never gave fright,

> he fought with the same courage in the shadow of death that he did in life.

# Ghetto Booty: The Hottentot Remix

*For Saartjie Baartman*

The spectacle wasn't you.
Look at them:

Men, without women, lining
the streets of cities to attend.

Same ones at the fray of Goree,
standing in shadows of the no-
return doorways.

*That was then,*

when you endured their "scientific" staccato,
trapped in the plaster of a fleshtone coffin
customized for cattle.

*That was then,*

When they sold ounces of your womanhood,
leaving you a weightless museum piece,
simply because they could.

*That was then,*
*Look at them.*

*That was them*
*Look at them.*

*That was then, and*

## Beautiful. And Ugly Too

I'm ashamed, only because, if *that was then,*
 – where was I, and the rest of our men?

Must have been studying *them,* for how to
treat daughters, scattered to Atlantic winds.

       We've become masters.

Spreading heteropsychotic donkey-rhythms
to those who were mastered.

And the masses think that the base-glossed vulture,
stalking the beauty of inverted brown wombs
for sales-jumps on posters,
is our culture.

So do we.

The spectacle is not them.
Look at us.

M.K. Asante, Jr.

# Missing

You ever seen battered
blacktop playgrounds, with
chains fronting as nets on

enslaved rims, standing quasi-
proud before underfunded
and overpopulated

concertina-corralled schools
with bars on subfusc
windows of class

rooms without computers, all
while she slaves shifts
of eight hours

to feed eight children under
one section-eight roof,
and for what?

# Miles Smiles (Circle)

Footprints racing,
timing my thoughts to the sweet
sounds of steel yams, straining
Blues for Pablo

Neruda,
while Art types piano
and I play the chord keyboard like
the Counts tap on a Blue Note floorboard.

Sing-a-song in that deep Weldon tenor,
slowing with each cherry-letter of electric
cities, & sounds lay scores to twenty-four
frames per second.

*It might could take a minute.*

# Elderly Race Leaders

*One negro who can talk more
bullshit than a fertilizer executive,
shake your hand fifty different
ways and still don't know nothin
bout common courtesy and bein
considerate.*

— Broadway

Is this the best we got?

Reminds me of Kansas City
cash stack sums, where a 20
note guards a tit wad of 1's.

The plot;

> to create a knot seemingly worth alot,
> named after Kansas City Slick, who,
> after years, eventually — got *got*.

Is this really the best we got?

# On the Poetree of Phyllis Wheatley: My Great, Great Babymomma

Is it possible to love the branches of a tree,
yet despise its roots?

You arrived wearing a carpet, it's fur
draped in soot.

It sat across your frame like a necklace
from the old country.

You left, but your poetree, inked in blood,
still haunts me.

Who was she; the dark girl with sad eyes?

Dunbar's babymomma.
Great Granddaughter of Sundiata.

  And my kin.

The ancestor of my grandfather's pen.

As far as her work:
  Tomorrow, I'll try again.

M.K. Asante, Jr.

# Clipped-Wing Birds

Clipped-wing birds
don't fly.

They

dance to
keep from falling;

laugh to
keep from crying;

pray to
keep from calling;

work to
keep from trying.

They

injure themselves
by not flying.

# Notes:

"A Libation in the Dark Tradition": The epigraph is an excerpt from Sun-Ra.

"Seeing Red": The epigraph is excerpted from *Notes on a Return to the Native Land* by Aimé Cesairé in which he coined the term Negritude.

"Zimbassippi": This poem owes much to *Echo of a Dumas-Storied Arkansippi Conch/us/nest* by Eugene B. Redmond.

"Luxury of Ignorance: Based on Shock and Awe": The latter part of this title is derived from *Shock & Awe: Achieving Rapid Dominance* by Harlan K. Ullman and James P. Wade. The passage reads:

> The basis for Rapid Dominance rests in the ability to affect the will, perception, and understanding of the adversary through imposing sufficient Shock and Awe to achieve the necessary political, strategic, and operational goals of the conflict or crisis that led to the use of force. War, of course, in the broadest sense has been characterized by Clausewitz to include substantial elements of fog, friction, and fear... He also observed that "war is deception," implying that Shock and Awe were greatly leveraged through clever, if not brilliant, employment of force.

"Fragrance of an Invisible Flower": The epigraph is excerpted from *The Drowned Book: Ecstatic and Earthy Reflections of Bhauddin, The Father of Rumi,* translated by Coleman Barks and John Moyne.

"The Spirit of Nkosi Johnson": The epigraph is excerpted from *We Are All The Same*, a speech by Nkosi Johnson. Nkosi, born with full-blown AIDS, was a valiant activist and educator who passed away at the age of twelve.

"The Master's Mother Tongue, Mastered by My Mother": The epigraph is excerpted from *The Tempest* by William Shakespeare.

"Beautiful. And Ugly Too": The title, also the title of this collection, is excerpted from *The Negro Artist and the Racial Mountain* by Langston Hughes, which first appeared in *The Nation* (1926). The passage reads:

> We younger Negro artists who create now intend to express our individual dark-skinned selves without fear or shame. If white people are pleased we are glad. If they are not, it doesn't matter. We know we are beautiful. And ugly too. The tom-tom cries and the tom-tom laughs. If colored people are pleased we are glad. If they are not, their displeasure doesn't matter either. We build our temples for tomorrow, strong as we know how, and we stand on top of the mountain, free within ourselves.

"One of the Ways God Must Taste": The epigraph is excerpted from *EHYEAH: A Kabbalah for Tomorrow* by Arthur Green.

"I am not that Random, America": This poem owes much to a series of conversations with Kenyan filmmaker Wanuri Kahui and Native American author Sherman Alexie.

"SAMO©": The title is drawn from Jean Michel Basquiat's graffiti name, SAMO© (Same Old Shit). Basquiat's anti-materialist tags proclaimed that "SAMO© was an end to mindwash religion, nowhere politics, and bogus philosophy," "SAMO© saves idiots," and "Plush safe he think; SAMO©".

"Live, Afrobohemian: A Tribute to Afrobohemianism": The epigraph is excerpted from a Sun-Ra interview which appeared in *Jazztalk* by Robert D. Rusch.

"Ghetto Booty: The Hottentot Remix": Saartjie Baartman (also known as Venus Hottentot), the poem's dedicatee, was a Khoisan woman who was taken from South Africa in 1810 by a British naval surgeon and, under the voyeuristic eye of the European public, forced to exhibit her buttocks at circus sideshows, museums, bars, and universities. Forced into prostitution, she died six years later at the age of 26.

"Elderly Race Leaders": The epigraph is excerpted from *Sitting Pretty* by Al Young.

"Father": This poem owes much to the bible-influenced *Prayers for Dark People* by W.E.B. Du Bois.

"Public School": This poem is excerpted and reversed from J.D. Rockefeller's General Education Board's *Occasional Letter* by Frederick Gates, issued in 1904.

# About the Author

M.K. Asante, Jr., 23, was born in Harare, Zimbabwe, amid the second Chimurenga (uprising) and raised in Philadelphia, PA. He is the author of *Like Water Running Off My Back*, for which he received the Academy of American Poets Jean Corrie Prize. Widely anthologized, Asante Jr's. writings have appeared in the *Encyclopedia of Black Studies* and *USA Today*, among others. An MFA candidate at UCLA's School of Film and Television, Asante, Jr. wrote the screenplay and produced the multi- award-winning documentary *500 Years Later*.